IITT JUNIOR

7·8
LEVEL

International Interpretation &
Translation Test for Juniors

IITT JUNIOR: LEVEL 7-8

© 사단법인 국제통번역자원봉사단, 2019

1판 1쇄 인쇄__2019년 04월 01일
1판 1쇄 발행__2019년 04월 05일

지은이__사단법인 국제통번역자원봉사단
펴낸이__홍정표

펴낸곳__글로벌콘텐츠
　　　　등록__제 25100-2008-000024호

공급처__(주)글로벌콘텐츠출판그룹
　　　　대표__홍정표 **디자인**__김미미 **기획·마케팅**__노경민 이조은 이종훈
　　　　주소__서울특별시 강동구 풍성로 87-6(성내동) 1, 2층 **전화**__02-488-3280 **팩스**__02-488-3281
　　　　홈페이지__www.gcbook.co.kr

값 14,000원
ISBN 979-11-5852-235-3 13740

Learning English and practicing English are quite different in Korea. We have learned English as a school subject. But English is used as an important skills in the global society. We have a lot of chances to meet many English speaking people here and there. If we are not so good at communication skills in English, we face some difficulties. We have to find the best possible way to develop our communication skills.

In order to achieve this goal, students and teachers should do something different from book-based education. Students need to practice English as a language - not just for school tests in Korea. The need to read a lot of sentences aloud and practice saying them in conversational not only with their friends but also with naive English speakers.

In this course, students can find several different kinds of reading materials and essays. I do hope the students will not stop at reading and understanding this book, but also try to practice all materials with their friends and teachers. Try to play with the sentences without worrying about mistakes or faults. Just try to read the sentences as many times as possible untill you can read them very fast and fluently.

At last, you will find that you are able to read the sentences without watching every single word and understand the sentences without translating into Korean. Then you are ready to communicate in English. That is the real purpose of studying English and it can keep you become an English speaking person. Try to keep this practice untill you can use English as a communication tool.

In the first part, you may encounter very simple expressions with some familiar materials. I hope you can be accustomed to reading the materials aloud and repeating them several times until you can read and understand the materials without thinking about every word. Then you can make your own short sentences for yourself someday.

In the second part, you may find some more advanced reading materials and basic essays. They will develop you into better English speakers and writers. Using English in your daily life is very helpful to you. Most importantly, try your best to keep going with this book to the last page and you will know how to use basic English in common life.

Teachers can help their students to develop English and prepare for the IITT, International Interpretation & Translation Test. Students will take the test for interpretation and translation soon. They need to practice for dictation, listening, and translation into Korean or English composition. Finally, they will wite an English essay. They have to score over 80% to pass.

Good luck !

Table of Contents

IITT JUNIOR

International Interpretation & Translation Test for Juniors

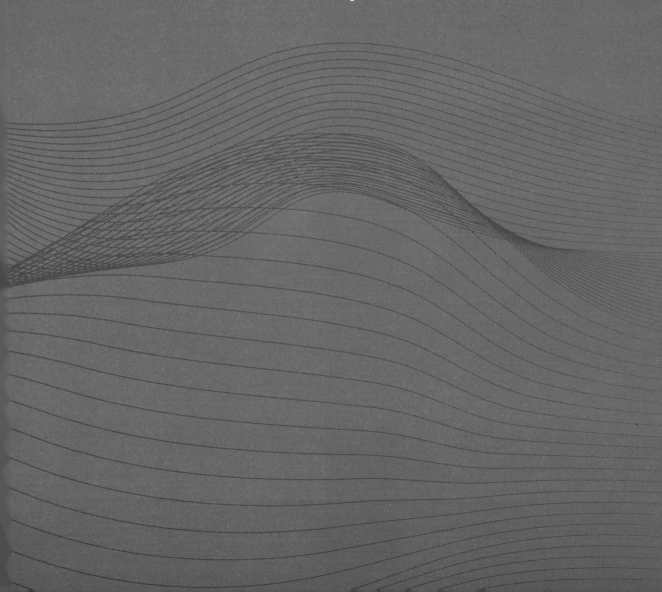

Unit 01

Introductions

My name is Jack Keegan.

Let me tell you about my school.

My school is located in Seoul, Korea.

I am a freshman at Seoul National College.

I like my school very much.

My school has some beautiful gardens.

We can see many flowers in the spring and enjoy the weather there.

I feel very good being with my classmates and teachers.

They are very kind and helpful.

I make a lot of new friends there too.

We usually eat lunch together and spend time during our breaks.

I like to play sports on campus and learn new things.

I can build my future here.

---

vocabulary

- locate: 위치하다, be situated(=be located)
- helpful: 도움이 되는(=useful)

1. Where is Jack's school?

   _____

2. What grade is he in now?

   _____

3. What does he like to do on campus?

   _____

1. My name is Jack Keegan.
   - I am Jack Keegan.
   - My full name is Jack Keegan.
   - You can call me Jack, short for Jack Keegan.

2. My school is located in Seoul, Korea.
   - My school's location is in Seoul, Korea.
   - My school is in Seoul, Korea.
   - You can find my school in Seoul, Korea.

3. I like my school very much.
   - I really like my school.
   - I really enjoy going to school.
   - I love my school very much.

Reorder the following words into correct sentences.

1. Let me (my / school / you / about / tell).

   _____

2. I like (very / much / my / school).

   _____

3. We can (many / see / in spring / flowers).

   _____

Choose the correct word or phrase.

1. Let me (to tell, tell) you about my school.

2. My school is (locating, located) in Seoul Korea.

3. My school (have, has) some beautiful gardens.

4. We can see (many, much) flowers in spring.

5. They (are, is) very kind and helpful.

6. I like (play. to play) sports.

7. I can (to make. make) my future here.

Laura usually gets up at 7:00 in the morning.

She has breakfast at 7:30 after washing her face.

She eats cereal and fruit for breakfast.

She changes clothes for school.

She goes to school by bus.

She usually has 5 or 6 classes a day.

She has some time to talk with her friends after school.

After doing her homework, she likes to hang out with her friends.

After dinner, Laura enjoys watching television.

Before going to bed, Laura likes to read books.

She goes to bed at 10:30.

And, upon waking up the next day, her routine starts again.

---

vocabulary

- by: ~로(방법, 수단), by bus, by train, by taxi
- after school: 방과후에
- routine: (판에 박힌) 일상

1. What time does Laura have breakfast?

   _____

2. What does she do after homework?

   _____

3. What does she do before going to bed?

   _____

1. Laura usually gets up at 7:00 in the morning.
   - Laura often gets up at 7:00 in the morning.
   - Laura gets up at 7:00 in the morning most of the time.
   - Laura regularly gets up at 7:00 in the morning.

2. She goes to school by bus.
   - She goes to school on a bus.
   - She rides a bus to go to school.
   - She takes a bus to go to school.

3. She goes to bed at 10:30.
   - She sleeps at 10:30.
   - She gets in bed at 10:30.
   - She falls asleep at 10:30.

Reorder the following words into correct sentences.

1. She goes (bed / 10:30 / at / to).

   _____

2. She changes (school / for / clothes).

   _____

3. She likes (her / to / with / hang out / friends).

   _____

Sentence Check

Choose the correct word or phrase.

1. Laura usually (get, gets) up at 7:00 in the morning.

2. She (eating, eats) cereal and fruit for breakfast.

3. She goes to school (with, by) bus.

4. She usually has 6 (classes, class) a day.

5. After doing her homework, she likes to (hang out, hanging out) with her friends.

6. After dinner, Laura enjoys (watching, to watch) television.

7. Before (go, going) to bed, Laura likes to read books.

What do you usually do during the weekend?

I really enjoy the weekend. Every week, I look forward to it. When Friday comes, I always shout, "T.G.I.F.!"

Last weekend, I spent time with my friends and family.

On Saturday, I went downtown with my best friend, Jin. First, we ate lunch together. We ate bulgogi pizza. That is my favorite topping. Next, we went to the arcade. Jin is really good at billiards. He was the winner most of the time, but that is okay because we had a great time.

On Sunday, I spent time with my family. We went to the park together. We took a walk and had a picnic. My mother prepared kimbap. It was so delicious! Then, my father, younger brother, and I played soccer. I scored the most goals!

I enjoy spending time with the people I am close to on the weekend. It is time to have fun and also rest. It helps me to feel fresh for the next week!

＊**T.G.I.F. - Thank God, it's Friday**

Write a short essay that answers the question:

– What did you do last weekend?

_____

_____

_____

_____

_____

_____

_____

_____

_____

_____

_____

_____

_____

_____

Unit 02

Plants

There are many kinds of flowers in the garden.

Flowers usually smell good and have beautiful colors.

Some flowers are red, others yellow, and some others white.

People buy flowers when they go to the hospital.

Flowers can make patients be relaxed and happy.

Flowers have their own names such as roses, lilies, and forget-me-nots.

People like to receive flowers on some special days.

Many couples give and receive flowers for their anniversary.

I especially like red roses.

I want to get red roses on my birthday.

vocabulary

- forget-me-nots: 물망초
- anniversary: 기념일

1. What do flowers have in common?

   _____

2. When do we need to buy flowers?

   _____

3. What is the write's favorite flower?

   _____

1. There are many kinds of flowers in the garden.
   - There are different kinds of flowers in the garden.
   - There are various kinds of flowers in the garden.
   - Many kinds of flowers are in the garden.

2. People like to receive flowers on some special days.
   - People like to receive flowers on some occasions.
   - People like to receive flowers on some special events.
   - People like to receive flowers on some special affairs.

3. I want to get red roses on my birthday.
   - I want to get red roses on my graduation.
   - I want to get red roses on our anniversary.
   - I want to get red roses on New Year's Day.

Reorder the following words into correct sentences.

1. Flowers can (happy / make / patients).

   _____

2. People like (flowers/ to/ on/ receive/ special days).

   _____

3. There are (many / of/ kinds / in the garden / flowers).

   _____

Choose the correct word or phrase.

1. There (is, are) many kinds of flowers in the garden.

2. (Any, Some) flowers are red.

3. People (buy, buys) flowers when they go to the hospital.

4. Flowers can (make, makes) patients happy.

5. I especially (likes, like) red roses.

6. People like (receive, to receive) flowers on special days.

7. I want (get, to get) red roses on my birthday.

We can see trees here and there.

Most trees are on the mountain.

Some trees are on the sides of the street.

Others are in the yard of a house.

Trees are very important for people.

Trees give us oxygen to breathe with.

We get fresh air to breathe from trees.

People can use trees for decoration.

People can build houses with wood from trees.

People collect unusual trees as a hobby.

People can even change the shape of a tree with tools.

---

vocabulary

- here and there: 여기저기에(서)
- breathe: 호흡하다, 냄새를 풍기다

1. Where can we find trees?

   _____

2. What can we do with trees?

   _____

3. Where can we get fresh air?

   _____

1. We can see tress here and there.
   - We can see trees everywhere.
   - We can see trees around us.
   - We can see trees anywhere.

2. We get fresh air to breathe from trees.
   - We get fresh air to inhale from trees.
   - We get fresh air to draw in from trees.
   - We get clean air to breathe from trees.

3. People can build houses with wood from trees.
   - Houses can be built with wood from trees.
   - With wood from trees, people can build houses.
   - Trees provide wood that can be used to build houses.

Reorder the following words into correct sentences.

1. Flowers some trees are (the sides / the street / on / of).

   _____

2. Others are (the yard / a house / in / of).

   _____

3. Trees are (for / very / people / important).

   _____

Sentence Check

Choose the correct word or phrase.

1. Most trees (are, is) on the mountain.

2. Others (is, are) in the yard of a house.

3. We can (builds, build) houses with wood from trees.

4. People (is, collect) unusual trees for pleasure.

5. Trees give (we, us) oxygen.

6. We (need, needs) air to breathe.

7. People can (using, use) trees for decoration.

The Importance of Plants

Plants are all around us. Everywhere we look, we can see flowers, grass, and trees. They are beautiful to look at and usually smell wonderful. Plants are very useful in our lives.

First, plants give us food. Vegetables and fruits come from plants. They have a lot of vitamins and fiber. They are very nutritious and good for our health. We can eat them raw, but they are used in cooking as well. Also, they are really delicious!

Second, plants are used to make many medicines. For example, Aloe Vera is very good for our skin and teeth. Some doctors say it is also good for our memory and learning. Another medicinal plant is garlic. Eating lots of garlic protects us from getting sick from colds and other viruses. Koreans have a lot of garlic in our diet because we love to eat kimchi!

In conclusion, plants help our lives in many ways. They give us tasty foods to eat and keep our body healthy. Plants are amazing and very important for all people!

Write a short essay that answers the question:

– Why do we need plants?

_____

_____

_____

_____

_____

_____

_____

_____

_____

_____

_____

_____

Seasons

Summer is the hottest time of the year in Korea.

It is a time to swim at the beach and play outdoors.

Children usually like this season the most.

Most schools don't have classes in summer.

Many students want to go on a trip to cool places.

It rains a lot and is humid in Korea.

Nights are often hot too.

A bad thing about the summer is the mosquitoes.

People sometimes get too hot and wait for the cool weather.

Others enjoy the warmth.

Most people enjoy having a long holiday during the summer.

---

vocabulary

- outdoors: 옥외에서, (도시를 벗어난)전원
- humid: 습한
- mosquito: 모기

1. What do we do in summer to feel cool?

   _____

2. What is good in summer?

   _____

3. How is the weather now?

   _____

Substitution Drills

1. Summer is the hottest time of the year.
   - The hottest time of the year is summer.
   - Summer is the boiling season time of the year.
   - Summer is a really scorching time of the year.

2. It rains a lot and is humid in Korea.
   - There are a lot of rains and is humid in Asia.
   - It rains a lot and is damp in Korea.
   - Asia is humid and it also rains a lot.

3. A bad thing about the summer is the mosquitoes.
   - A negative thing about the summer is the mosquitoes.
   - A disadvantage of summer is the mosquitoes.
   - Mosquitoes is a bad thing about summer.

Reorder the following words into correct sentences.

1. Children usually like (season / this / the most).

   _____

2. Nights are (hot / often / too).

   _____

3. People sometimes get too hot and wait (the cool / weather / for).

   _____

Sentence Check

Choose the correct word or phrase.

1. Summer is (the hottest, the hotter) time of the year.

2. It is a time (swim, to swim) at the beach and play outdoors.

3. It (rains, rain) a lot and (are, is) humid in Asia.

4. A bad thing about the summer (are, is) the mosquitoes.

5. Most people enjoy (have, having) a long holiday during the summer.

6. Most schools (doesn't, don't) have classes.

7. Many students want (goes, to go) on a trip to cool places.

Fall is many people's favorite season.

The leaves on the trees change colors.

The colors are very beautiful.

Many people visit the mountains in fall.

They want to enjoy the cool air and the beautiful scenery.

Some people think that fall is the best time to read books.

Farmers are usually busy harvesting crops.

There are a lot of fruits in the orchard.

Some people are waiting for the coming winter.

They look forward to seeing the snow soon.

Kids are waiting for snowy days, too.

---

vocabulary

- scenery: 경치, 풍경, (무대의)배경, 무대장치
- harvest: 수확하다. 거둬들이다.
- crop: (농)작물, (한 철에 거둔)수확량.
- orchard: 과수원.

1. What happens to the leaves of the trees in fall?

   _____

2. What do people usually do in fall?

   _____

3. What can you see in the mountain during autumn?

   _____

1. The colors are very beautiful.
   - The colors are stunning.
   - The shades are striking.
   - The tints are magnificent.

2. Many people visit the mountains in fall.
   - In fall, many people visit the mountains.
   - In fall, the mountains are a popular place to visit.
   - A lot of people go to the mountains in fall.

3. They look forward to seeing the snow soon.
   - They anticipate seeing the snow soon.
   - They are excited to see the snow soon.
   - They look forward to seeing snowflakes soon.

Reorder the following words into correct sentences.

1. Fall is (season / for/ the favorite / people / many).

   _____

2. Some people think that (fall / time / is / to read / the best / books).

   _____

3. Some people are (winter / waiting / the coming / for).

   _____

Sentence Check

Choose the correct word or phrase.

1. The leaves (in, on) the trees change colors.

2. Many people visit the mountains (in, on) fall.

3. They want (enjoy, to enjoy) the cool air and the beautiful scenery.

4. Farmers are usually busy (harvest, harvesting) crops.

5. There are a lot of fruits (in, about) the orchard.

6. They look forward to (see, seeing) the snow soon.

7. Kids are waiting (in, for) snowy days too.

In your opinion, which season is the best in your country?

Korea has four seasons. Spring, summer, fall, and winter come every year. Everyone has a favorite season they enjoy the most. In my opinion, spring is the best season in Korea.

Firstly, spring has the best weather. The temperature is mostly warm and sometimes cool. It is usually sunny with a little rain here and there. Spring is a great time to enjoy the outdoors. People like taking walks and having picnics in spring. Summer is much too hot and humid. Winter is too cold and snowy.

Also, spring is the most beautiful season. Flowers bloom in spring. There are wonderful colors and smells everywhere. Animals come out from their winter sleep and the world is full of life. In Korea, people especially enjoy the cherry blossoms in spring. There are many festivals celebrating their beauty.

In summary, spring is my favorite season. Every year, the seasons come and go. When winter passes and the birds and flowers appear, I always feel very happy!

Lesson 4   Essay Practice

Write a short essay that answers the question:

– What season do you like best and why?

_____

_____

_____

_____

_____

_____

_____

_____

_____

_____

_____

_____

_____

Pets

Dogs are considered to be man's best friend.

Dogs are loyal and loving to their owners.

Dogs can feel love and emotional pain much like humans.

They also like to play and have fun.

They can help them walk.

Some people train dogs for special purposes.

They can help hunt other wild animals or even detect drugs.

Dogs are useful for the blind.

Dogs even live in our homes and sleep with us in our bedrooms.

People like dogs for many reasons.

vocabulary

- consider: (~을 ~로)여기다, 고려하다
- loyal: 충실한, 충성스러운(=true)
- emotional: 정서의, 감정의, 감정을 자극하는
- like: ~와 비슷한, ~같은
- purpose: 목적, 용도, 의도
- detect: (특히 알아내기 어려운 것을) 발견하다, 알아내다

1. What can dogs do for his owner?

   _____

2. Where does a pet dog live?

   _____

3. What kind of pet dog do you know?

   _____

1. Dogs are considered to be man's best friend.
   - Dogs are regarded to be man's best friend.
   - Dogs are believed to be man's best friend.
   - Man considers dogs as their best friend.
2. Some people train dogs for special purposes.
   - Dogs are trained (by people) for special purposes.
   - Training of dogs is for special purposes.
   - There are special purposes some people train dogs.
3. People like dogs for many reasons.
   - People adore dogs for many reason.
   - People like dogs because of a lot of things.
   - Dogs are liked by people for many reasons.

Reorder the following words into correct sentences.

1. Dogs are (their owners / to / loyal and / loving).

   _____

2. Some people train (special / dogs / for / purposes).

   _____

3. People like (many / for / reasons / dogs).

   _____

Choose the correct word or phrase.

1. Dogs are (considering, considered) to be man's best friend.

2. Dogs can (feeling, feel) love and emotional pain much like humans.

3. Dogs are (using, useful) for the blind.

4. They can (help to help) them walk.

5. They can help (hunt, hunted) other animals or even detect drugs.

6. Dogs even (living, live) in our homes and sleep with us in our bedrooms.

Cats are very common pets in most of the world.

They are very different from dogs.

Cats are very independent.

They don't need the same care that dogs need.

They also can't be trained to do things like a dog.

Cats are often mysterious.

That is a part of their charm.

Most people don't like wild cats on the street.

We can see cute cats in movies.

We can see some cats in horror movies as well.

Cats can have two sides to people.

They are a symbol of both cuteness and evil.

---

vocabulary

- independent: 독립된, 자립적인
- mysterious: 이해하기 힘든, 기이한, 신비한
- cuteness: 귀염성
- evil: 사악한, 유해한

1. What are the differences between dogs and cats?

    _____

2. What are wild cats?

    _____

3. Why do people think of cats as cute pets?

    _____

1. Cats are very common pets in most of the world.
    - Cats are typical pets in most of the world.
    - Cats are very usual pets in most of the world.
    - Cats are very common domesticated animals in the world.

2. They also can't be trained to do things like a dog.
    - They also aren't able to be trained to do things like a dog.
    - They can't be trained to do things unlike a dog.
    - They are dissimilar to a dog because they can't be trained to do things.

3. Most people don't like wild cats on the street.
    - Wild cats on the street aren't liked (by most people).
    - Most people dislike wild cats on the street.
    - Most people detest wild cats on the street.

Reorder the following words into correct sentences.

1. Most people don't (wild cats / like / on the street).

   _____

2. They also can't (trained/ to do/ be/ like a dog/ things).

   _____

3. We can see (in horror / some cats / movies / as well).

   _____

Choose the correct word or phrase.

1. They are very different (in, from) dogs.

2. They don't need the same care that dogs (need, needs).

3. They also can't (are, be) trained to do things like a dog.

4. That is a part (at, of) their charm.

5. We can see (cute, cutely) cats in movies.

6. Also, we can (see, seeing) some cats in horror movies as well.

7. Cats are a symbol (of, for) both cuteness and evil.

What is your favorite pet and why?

Dogs and cats are probably the most popular kinds of pets. A lot of families have either a dog or a cat. Sometimes, they have both! I think dogs are great pets, but I prefer cats for the following reasons.

First, cats are easy to take care of. Cats don't need so much attention. They don't need to go for walks or go outside very often. They are very clean and usually don't need a bath. They are very smart and don't need a lot of training.

Second, they are very cute. Cats have big, beautiful eyes and small faces. They have short fur that can be many different colors. They love to play with balls or pieces of string. When you pet them they purr to show that they are happy.

To review, cats are my kind of pet. I prefer them to dogs because they are easier to take care of and are very loveable and cute. I think most people prefer dogs, but I am proud to be called a "cat person."

Write a short essay that answers the question:

– Which do you prefer, dogs or cats? Give at least two reasons.

_____

_____

_____

_____

_____

_____

_____

_____

_____

_____

_____

_____

_____

Unit 05

Special Days

Around 2000 years ago, a baby was born in Jerusalem.

His name was Jesus.

People said he was the single son of God.

Many people called him the Lord.

He did a lot of great things during his life.

Many people followed him to learn his wisdom.

He had 12 good students who followed him.

After he was killed by the King of Rome, he came back to life.

He was honored by people all around the world.

Christians began to celebrate his birth. We call the day "Christmas."

This is a special day, so most people celebrate it with their families, friends, or lovers.

People also exchange gifts on Christmas Day.

They have parties and gatherings during this day.

---

vocabulary

- wisdom: 지혜
- goal: 목표
- revive: 회복하다, 부활시키다
- honor: 명예, 영예, 체면

1. What did people call Jesus?

   _____

2. Why did people follow Jesus?

   _____

3. What do people do on Christmas?

   _____

1. He had 12 good students who followed him.
   - He had 12 good pupils who followed him.
   - He had 12 disciples who followed him.
   - He had 12 apostles for who followed him.

2. After he was killed by the King of Rome, he revived.
   - After he was killed by the King of Rome, he came back to life.
   - After he was killed by the King of Rome, he was resurrected.
   - After he was killed by the King of Rome, he was restored to life.

3. People also exchange gifts on Christmas Day.
   - Gifts are exchanged (by people) on Christmas Day.
   - People also exchange presents on Christmas Day.
   - People give each other presents on Christmas Day.

Reorder the following words into correct sentences.

1. People said (the single / son of God / he was).

   _____

2. He had (12 / students / who / him / followed).

   _____

3. People exchange (on / gifts / Christmas day).

   _____

Choose the correct word or phrase.

1. Around 2000 years ago, a baby was (bear, born) in Jerusalem.

2. Many people (calls, called) him the Lord.

3. He (does, did) a lot of great things during his life.

4. Many people (follows, followed) him to learn his wisdom.

5. After he was (kill, killed) by the King of Rome, he came back to life.

6. He was (honors, honored) by the people all around the world.

7. Christians began (celebrate, to celebrate) his birth.

Lesson 2　Korea's Independence Day

In 1910, Japan invaded Korea.

The Japanese controlled Korea by force for 36 years.

During that time, many Koreans were killed by the Japanese.

However, Koreans never gave up the dream of independence.

They tried to restore the power of the country.

On the 15th of August in 1945, Japan collapsed.

The Japanese went back to their country.

Koreans remember that day and their ancestors who fought against Japan.

They sacrificed their lives during the colonial time.

Koreans celebrate that day as their Independence Day on the 15th of August every year.

Many Asian countries have achieved their independences from Japan at the same time.

---

vocabulary

- invade: 침범하다.
- give up: 포기하다(=abondon)
- restore: 회복시키다. 복원하다.
- collapse: 무너지다. 붕괴하다.
- sacrifice: 희생하다. 희생시키다.

1. How long did Japan colonize Korea?

   _____

2. When did Japan collapse?

   _____

3. What did Koreans do for their country?

   _____

1. In 1910, the Japanese invaded Korea.
   - In 1910, Korea was invaded by the Japanese.
   - The Japanese invaded Korea in 1910.
   - Korea was invaded by the Japanese in 1910.

2. However, Koreans never gave up the dream of independence.
   - Nevertheless, Koreans never gave up the dream of independence.
   - However, Koreans never surrendered the dream of independence.
   - However, Koreans never gave up the dream of liberty.

3. The Japanese went back to their country.
   - The Japanese returned to their country.
   - The Japanese retreated to their country.
   - The Japanese withdrew to their country.

Reorder the following words into correct sentences.

1. The Japanese controlled (by / Korea / force / 45 years / for).

_____

2. On the (1945/ in/ of August / 15th), Japan collapsed.

_____

3. Koreans remember that day and their ancestors (against / fought / who / Japan).

_____

Choose the correct word or phrase.

1. In 1910, the Japanese (invaded, invade) Korea.

2. During that time, (many, much) Koreans were killed by the Japanese.

3. They tried (restore, to restore) the power of the country.

4. The Japanese (goes, went) back to their country.

5. They sacrificed their lives (during, at) the colonial time.

6. Koreans (celebrating, celebrate) the day as their independence day.

7. (Much, Many) Asian countries achieved independence from Japan at the same time.

What is your favorite holidays?

We all look forward to holidays. They are a time to meet family and friends. We can eat delicious food and play fun games. We can remember and celebrate important events from the past. I will describe a special day in Korea called Parents' Day.

To start, Parents' Day is on May 8th of every year in Korea. On this day we honor our parents and thank them for everything they do for us. Our parents work very hard to make our lives better. So, on this day, we give them a carnation and show our love and appreciation.

Last Parents' Day, our family had a lot of fun. My older brother and I gave my mother a beautiful red carnation. For our father, we bought a cool tie and a pair of socks. We also made cards at school for our parents. We wrote a special message in the cards. In the evening, we all went out for dinner at my mother's favorite Italian restaurant.

Every year May 8th in Korea, we have a special day for our parents. I think it is a very important day because our parents do so much for us. They want us to become hardworking and kind people. Every Parents' Day, I make sure they know I appreciate them!

Write a short essay about:

- A special day that you know

_____

_____

_____

_____

_____

_____

_____

_____

_____

_____

_____

_____

_____

_____

Unit 06

School Subjects

We start to study English in elementary school.

However, studying English is not easy for students.

Particularly, it is difficult for them to speak English.

I try to pay attention in my English class.

I try to remember words and sentences every day.

I read English books aloud at home.

I speak English with my English teacher.

He is from Canada.

He is very kind and helpful.

He explains essential words and fun idioms.

Nowadays, English is becoming my favorite subject.

I will become good at English soon.

English is a global language.

So, I think being able to express myself in English is vital.

---

vocabulary

- pay attention to: ~에 유의하다, ~에 주목하다
- essential: 필수적인(=vital), 본질적인(=fundamental)
- idion: 관용구, 숙어

1. When did you start to learn English?

   _____

2. Where does your English teacher come from?

   _____

3. What can we do to improve English at home?

   _____

1. I try to pay attention in my English class.

   - I try to listen in my English class.

   - I try to be attentive in my English class.

   - In my English class, I try to pay attention.

2. He explains essential words and fun idioms.

   - He teaches essential words and fun idioms.

   - He explains important words and fun idioms.

   - He explains useful words and fun phrases.

3. I will become good at English soon.

   - I will get better at English soon.

   - Soon, I will become good at English

   - I will improve my English skills soon.

Reorder the following words into correct sentences.

1. I try (to pay / my English / in / attention / class).

   _____

2. I (speak / English / my / with / teacher).

   _____

3. English is (language / a / global).

   _____

Choose the correct word or phrase.

1. We start to study English (in, on) elementary school.

2. However, studying English is not easy (at, for) me.

3. Particularly, it is difficult (by, for) me to speak English.

4. I read English books aloud (at, for) home.

5. He is (of, from) Canada.

6. English is (become, becoming) my favorite subject nowadays.

7. I will become good (at, in) English soon.

When I was young, I wanted to become a scientist.

I liked Thomas Edison very much.

I read a book about him last year.

Edison invented the light bulb and motion pictures.

I saw many intriguing things at The Science World in Vancouver.

I am interested in biology and chemistry.

I like to learn about the human body.

We can learn fascinating things from our science teacher.

Science is an interesting subject.

Many things can be discovered and changed by scientist.

Scientists have invented many things that make the world more convenient.

Inventions such as electricity, cars, and computers have changed our lives.

---

vocabulary

- intrigning: (분명한 해답이 없고 특이해서) 아주 흥미로운
- biology: 생물학
- chemistry: 화학
- convenient: 편리한, (~에) 가까운

1. What can scientists do for the world?

   _____

2. Who invented motion pictures?

   _____

3. What are the branches of science that you know?

   _____

1. I am interested in biology and chemistry.
   - I am passionate about biology and chemistry.
   - I am keen on biology and chemistry.
   - I am into biology and chemistry.

2. Scientists have invented many convenient things for the world.
   - Many convenient things for the world have been invented by scientists.
   - Scientists have made many convenient things for the world.
   - Scientists have created many convenient things for the world.

3. Inventions such as electricity, cars, and computers have changed our lives.
   - Our lives have changed because of inventions such as ~
   - Inventions such as ~ have altered our lives.
   - Inventions such as ~ have made our lives better.

Reorder the following words into correct sentences.

1. I read (last year / him / a book / about).

   _____

2. Edison invented (and motion / the light bulb / pictures).

   _____

3. I am (biology and / interested / chemistry/ in).

   _____

Sentence Check

Choose the correct word or phrase.

1. When I was young, I wanted (become, to become) a scientist.

2. Science (are, is) an interesting subject.

3. (Much, Many) things can be changed by a scientist.

4. I saw (much, many) intriguing things at The Science World in Vancouver.

5. I like to learn (about, at) the human body.

6. We can learn (some, any) fascinating things from our science teacher.

7. Inventions such as electricity, cars, and computers have (change, changed) our lives.

Describe one school subject.

In Korea, English is a foreign language. However, it is a mandatory subject in school. Students here study English from kindergarten to university. It is one of the most important things we study. For me, English is also the most useful school subject.

In the first place, English can help us communicate globally. The international language used for most communication is English whether it be for business or just everyday conversation. English is usually the language of choice for cross-cultural exchange. People all over the world study and practice English.

Furthermore, English can help us find jobs. In Korea, most large companies and government offices require an English interview or English essay. Many employers give tests for translation and interpretation skills. There are also many English proficiency tests that give a score for our English ability.

As a result, being good at English is very useful. My dream is to become an English interpreter and translator for a multi-national company or for the Korean government. The world is becoming smaller every day and English is a global language.

Write a short essay that answers the question:

- Which school subject do you think is the most useful to you and why?

_____

_____

_____

_____

_____

_____

_____

_____

_____

_____

_____

_____

Teacher's Comment

Unit 07

Relationships

A best friend is someone who can make you happy.

A best friend is also there for you when you need him the most.

A best friend can make you feel better when you are down.

A best friend can share his happiness with you.

I have a good friend at school.

His name is Tom Wells.

He is as tall as I am and very smart.

He is good at many subjects and sports.

He is very popular among our peers.

He and I have similar hobbies.

After school, we go to the park and play ball together.

I always feel happy with him

We promised that if we ever get separated in the future, we will make sure to maintain the friendship that we have built.

---

vocabulary

- share: 공유하다, 나누다
- popular: 인기있는, 대중적인
- peer: 또래
- maintain: 유지하다(=preserve), 주장하다(=insist)

1. How is a best friend described in the reading above?

   _____

2. Who is your best friend? Describe him or her in detail.

   _____

3. What do you usually do with your best friend?

   _____

1. A best friend can share his happiness with you.
   - Happiness can be shared with a best friend.
   - Your best friend's happiness can be shared with you.
   - Your best friend can share his happiness with you.

2. He is very popular among our peers.
   - Among our peers, he is very popular.
   - His popularity among our peers is high.
   - He is likeable among our peers.

3. After school, we go to the park and play ball together.
   - We go to the park and play ball together after school.
   - Together, we go to the park and play ball after school.
   - When classes end, we go to the park and play ball together.

Reorder the following words into correct sentences.

1. A best friend can (his happiness / with / share / you).

   _____

2. A best friend is also (for you / there / when you / the most / need him).

   _____

3. (I / He / have / and) similar hobbies.

   _____

Choose the correct word or phrase.

1. A best friend is someone (which, who) can make you happy.

2. A best friend can make feel better (what, when) you are down.

3. He is as tall (than, as) me and very smart.

4. He is good (in, at) many subjects and sports.

5. He is very popular (from, among) our peers.

6. After school, we (goes, go) to the park and play ball together.

7. I always (feel, feeling) happy with him.

During our school years, we become close to certain teachers.

These teachers usually teach certain subjects that we like.

Our favorite teacher is someone who we admire and wish to be like.

I like my math teacher the most.

His name is Mr. Smith.

He is handsome and very gentle.

When we don't understand a lesson, he explains it again.

Even though I make mistakes on some problems, he shows me the process.

When I meet him at school, I want to greet him every time.

He shows us some magic in class.

Most of my friends like him very much.

I think it is important that a teacher is both smart and friendly.

<u>**vocabulary**</u>

- admire: 존경하다, 감탄하며 바라보다
- magic: 마술

1. Describe Mr. Smith.

   _____

2. Who is your favorite teacher?

   _____

3. Why do you like him or her? Tell me something about that teacher.

   _____

Substitution Drills

1. I like my math teacher the most.
   - My favorite teacher is my math teacher.
   - I really like my math teacher more than my other teachers.
   - I really admire my math teacher the most.

2. He is handsome and very gentle.
   - He is good-looking and very gentle.
   - He has a handsome face and a gentle personality.
   - He is attractive inside and out.

3. Most of my friends like him very much.
   - He is very much liked by most of my friends.
   - Many of my friends like him very much.
   - Most of my friends admire him a lot.

Reorder the following words into correct sentences.

1. When I meet him at school, (I / greet / every time / him / want to).

   _____

2. Our favorite teacher is someone (we admire / and / who / wish / to be like).

   _____

3. When we don't understand a lesson, (explains / he / again / it).

   _____

Sentence Check

Choose the correct word or phrase.

1. (For, During) our school years, we become close to certain teachers.

2. These teachers usually (teaching, teach) certain subjects that we like.

3. I like my math teacher the (more, most).

4. When we don't understand his lesson, he explains (it, them) again.

5. Even (though, although) I make a mistake on some problems, he shows me the process.

6. He shows (we, us) some magic in class.

7. Most of my friends like (he, him) very much.

Talk about one family member.

My family consists of my father, mother, little sister, and me. I love my family very much. They are all very special to me. My little sister is 11 years old and her name is Cindy. Now, I will tell you about my little sister.

To begin with, she is very smart. She likes to go to school and study. This is amazing to me because I don't like studying very much. She even likes to do homework! She reads books all the time and is really good at English.

Also, she is very generous. She always shares her food with her friends. She makes sure to help my mother and father with housework. She usually helps my mom do the dishes after dinner. On my birthday, she bought me a new soccer ball with the money she saved!

In summary, I am really proud of my sister. I know she will be a great person in the future. I am really lucky to have a little sister like Cindy.

Write a short essay about:

- One of your family members

_____

_____

_____

_____

_____

_____

_____

_____

_____

_____

_____

_____

Unit 08

Great People

King Sejong was one of the greatest kings in Korean history.

He is also one of the best known and respected.

He is remembered mainly for the creation of the Korean alphabet.

He wanted to create the letters of the Korean language.

Koreans used to see Chinese characters to write their language.

It was difficult for Koreans to write and speak Chinese.

King Sejong gathered a group of scholars to invent the Korean alphabet.

Finally, he created 28 Korean letters.

It was called Hangeul.

After it was invented, it was changed a few times.

The Korean language has 24 characters now.

Hangeul is now known as an alphabet that is easy to read and write.

<u>vocabulary</u>

- respect: 존경, 경의
- creation: 창조, 창작

1. Who invented Korean alphabet characters?

2. What did Koreans use before Hangeul?

3. How many characters are there in Korean alphabet today?

1. King Sejong was one of the greatest Kings in Korean history.
   - One of the greatest kings in Korean history was King Sejong.
   - In Korean history, King Sejong was one of the greatest kings.
   - There were a lot of great kings in Korean history, and one of them was King Sejong.

2. King Sejong gathered a group of men to invent a Korean alphabet.
   - He brought together a group of men to invent a Korean alphabet.
   - He invited a group of men to invent a Korean alphabet.
   - He chose a group of men to create a Korean alphabet

3. The Korean language has 24 characters now.
   - Hanguel has 24 characters now.
   - There are now 24 characters in the Korean language.
   - Today, the Korean Language has 24 characters.

Reorder the following words into correct sentences.

1. King Sejong was (one / in Korean history / of the greatest / kings).

   _____

2. It was difficult (Koreans / for / write / to) and speak Chinese.

   _____

3. Koreans used (to write / Chinese / language / characters / their/ to use).

   _____

Choose the correct word or phrase.

1. He is also one of the best (now, known) and respected.

2. He is (remember, remembered) mainly for the creation of the Korean alphabet.

3. He wanted to (create, created) the letters of the Korean language.

4. He gathered a group of men (to invent, invent) a Korean alphabet.

5. Finally he (invented, invents) 28 a Korean alphabet.

6. After it was invented, it was (changed, change) a little.

7. Hangeul is now known (by, as) a language that is easy to read and write.

Helen Keller

Helen Keller was born in 1880 in a small town in America.

She was both blind and deaf because of a serious fever.

That meant she couldn't see or hear anything.

Despite these handicaps, she remained a happy and bright person.

Her reputation was thanks to the help of a good teacher named Anne Sullivan.

Anne didn't let Helen's disabilities depress her.

Instead, she helped Helen find ways to enjoy her life.

Although Anne had very weak sight as well. She read books to Helen

Helen improved the lives of other disabled people.

Many people admire her.

She was a great writer in American history.

---

vocabulary

- blind: 눈이 먼, 맹인인
- deaf: 청각장애가 있는, 귀가 먹은
- handicap: (신체, 정신적) 장애(=disability)

1. What is Helen Keller's nationality?

   _____

2. What handicaps did Helen have?

   _____

3. Who is Anne Sullivan?

   _____

1. Helen Keller was born in 1880 in a small town in America.
   - In 1880, Helen Keller was born in a small town in America.
   - In a small town in America, Helen Keller was born in 1880.
   - In 1880, in a small town in America, Helen Keller was born.

2. Instead, she helped Helen to find ways to enjoy her life.
   - Instead, she assisted Helen in finding ways to enjoy her life.
   - Instead, she aided Helen find ways to enjoy her life.
   - Instead, she guided Helen so that she could enjoy her life.

3. Helen improved the lives of other disabled people.
   - Helen improved the lives of other handicapped people.
   - Helen improved the lives of other people with disabilities.
   - The lives of other disabled people were improved by Helen.

Reorder the following words into correct sentences.

1. She was (blind / and / both / deaf/ a serious fever / because of).

   _____

2. She was (writer / in / a great / American / history).

   _____

3. Anne didn't (depress / Helen's disabilities / her).

   _____

Choose the correct word or phrase.

1. Helen Keller was (bear, born) in 1880 in a small town in America.

2. That meant she couldn't (see, saw) or hear anything.

3. Despite these handicaps, she (remained, is) a happy and bright person.

4. Her reputation was thanks (to, at) the help of a good teacher named Anne Sullivan.

5. Instead, she helped Helen (find, found) ways to enjoy her life.

6. Anne (had, has) very weak sight as well.

7. Helen improved the (life, lives) of other disabled people.

Who is Albert Einstein?

There have been many great people in history. I like to read about them and learn from their lives. A great person I admire is Albert Einstein

To begin, Albert Einstein was one the smartest people to ever live. He was a genius. He studied math and physics. He created the theory of relativity and won the Nobel Prize for physics in 1921.

To continue, Albert Einstein also wanted peace and equality for all people. He was against the nuclear weapon and he was very sad that science helped to make these horrible inventions. He also helped the African-Americans to have equal rights. Einstein was a Jew, so he helped his people in many ways too.

Albert Einstein was a great man that almost everyone knows. He had a brilliant mind and a loving heart. He is one of my heroes, and someone I look up to very much!

Write a short essay about:

- A great person you admire

_____

_____

_____

_____

_____

_____

_____

_____

_____

_____

_____

_____

_____

Unit 09

Food

Steak is a tender piece of meat taken from a cow.

It can be cooked rare, which means cooked just a little.

It can also be cooked medium, which means it is partially red inside and brown outside.

And, well done, which means it is cooked thoroughly.

Good steak restaurants are common throughout the world, where people enjoy eating.

Different kinds of steak are being served at restaurants.

There are rib, T-bone, and porterhouse steaks.

Commonly, steak means beef.

However, some cooks prepare steaks with fish or lamb.

Steaks are best when cooked on a charcoal grill.

<u>**vocabulary**</u>

- rare: 드문, 진귀한, 살짝익힌
- partially: 불완전하게, 부분적으로
- commonly: 흔히, 보통

1. How can steak be cooked?

   _____

2. How do you like your steak?

   _____

3. Where is your favorite steak house?

   _____

Substitution Drills

1. Steak is a tender piece of meat taken from a cow.
   - Steak is a soft piece of meat taken from a cow.
   - Steak is a tender piece of meat from a cow.
   - A tender piece of meat taken from a cow is called a steak.

2. Different kinds of steak are served at restaurants.
   - Restaurants serve different kinds of steak.
   - There are different kinds of steak served at restaurants.
   - An assortment of steaks is served at restaurants.

3. Commonly, steak means beef.
   - Most people know that steak means beef.
   - Steak commonly means beef.
   - Usually, steak means beef.

Reorder the following words into correct sentences.

1. Steak is (meat / piece of / taken from / a tender / a cow).

   _____

2. Good steak restaurants (the world / are / common / throughout).

   _____

3. It can also (medium / can / be cooked / also).

   _____

Choose the correct word or phrase.

1. It is (cook, cooked) rare, which means cooked a little.

2. It means cooked (thorough, thoroughly).

3. More and more kinds of steak are (serve, served) at restaurants.

4. Commonly, steak (are, means) beef.

5. Some (cooks, cookers) prepare steaks with fish or lamb.

6. Steaks are best when (cooking, cooked) on a charcoal grill.

7. Good steak restaurants are (coming, common) throughout the world.

Pizza is usually a good food for lunch and dinner.

Nobody knows exactly where the name came from.

Pizza consists of two main parts.

The first is a piece of bread in a round shape.

The other is the toppings on the pizza.

The kind of pizza depends on its toppings.

It is served in a variety of ways with many different kinds of toppings.

Many people visit a pizza restaurant to enjoy pizza.

But, some people cook pizza at home.

Pizza delivery is also popular.

A delivery place can take your order over the phone.

Your pizza will usually be delivered quickly, although not always.

<u>vocabulary</u>

• consist of: ~으로 이루어지다
• order: 주문, 순서, 질서

1. Describe the two parts of a pizza.

   _____

2. How often do you have pizza?

   _____

3. Do you have a favorite pizza restaurant? Where?

   _____

1. Pizza consists of two main parts.
   - Pizza has two main parts.
   - There are two main parts of pizza.
   - Pizza consists of two chief parts.

2. The first part is a piece of bread in a round shape.
   - The first part is a round shape piece of bread.
   - The first portion is a piece of bread in a round shape.
   - A piece of bread in a round shape is the first part of pizza.

3. A delivery place can take your order over the phone.
   - A delivery place can take your order by phone.
   - A delivery place can take your order through the phone.
   - Your order can be taken over the phone.

Reorder the following words into correct sentences.

1. Pizza consists (main / of / parts / two).

   _____

2. Many people visit (enjoy / a pizza / to / restaurant / pizza).

   _____

3. Pizza is (in a variety of / served / with many different / ways / kinds of toppings).

   _____

Choose the correct word or phrase.

1. Nobody knows exactly where the name came (in, from).

2. The first part is a piece of bread (for, in) a round shape.

3. The other are the toppings (in, on) the pizza.

4. The kind of pizza depends (for, on) its toppings.

5. Some people cook pizza (from, at) home.

6. A delivery place can take your order (over, in) the phone.

7. Your pizza will usually be (deliver, delivered) quickly, although not always.

What is your favorite food?

One of my favorite meals is scrambled eggs. It is a delicious and healthy meal made for breakfast or brunch. Best of all, scrambled eggs are fast and easy to cook.

First, you must crack a few eggs into a bowl. Then, add a pinch of salt and a little milk. The milk will make the eggs light and fluffy. You can whip the eggs with a spoon or fork. Make sure you whip the eggs really well for about 2 or 3 minutes.

Next, prepare a frying pan on medium heat with some butter. Pour the whipped eggs into the pan. As the eggs cook, use a spatula to lift and pull the eggs to make them scrambled.

Finally, put the scrambled eggs on a plate. You can add a little pepper to make it taste better. It is usually served with some toast and fruit.

Enjoy a wonderful meal!

Write a short essay that answers the question:

- How do you cook one of your favorite meals?

_____

_____

_____

_____

_____

_____

_____

_____

_____

_____

_____

_____

Unit 10

The Solar System

The moon is our closest neighbor in the universe.

It also influences the earth in many ways.

The moon influences the gravity of the earth.

It influences the tides in the ocean too.

It also affects the behavior of animals.

Some people have traveled to the moon.

Americans call them astronauts and Russians use the term cosmonauts.

Neil Armstrong was the first man to step on the moon.

The moon shines beautifully in the night sky.

It has many names such as Luna, Diana, or Artemis.

It is also named by its shape.

It can be called a full moon, a new moon, a half moon, or a harvest moon.

---

vocabulary

- influence: (사람의 행동·사고에) 영향을 주다(=affect)
- gravity: 중력
- astronaut: 우주비행사
- cosmonaut: (과거 러시아의) 우주비행사

1. What does the moon influence on earth?

   _____

2. Who was the first man on the moon?

   _____

3. What are some of the names given to the moon?

   _____

1. It also affects the behavior of animals.
   - It also has effects on the behavior of animals.
   - It also impacts the behavior of animals.
   - The behavior of animals is also affected.

2. Some people have traveled to the moon.
   - Some people have visited the moon.
   - Some people have been to the moon.
   - People have gone to the moon.

3. The moon shines beautifully in the night sky.
   - The moon gleams beautifully in the night sky.
   - The moon glows beautifully in the night sky.
   - The moon glimmers beautifully in the night sky.

Reorder the following words into correct sentences.

1. It also influences (many / the / in / earth / ways).

   _____

2. It also affects (animals / the / of / behavior).

   _____

3. The moon (in the / beautifully/ shines / night sky).

   _____

Sentence Check

Choose the correct word or phrase.

1. The moon is (we, our) closest neighbor in the universe.

2. The moon (influence, influences) the gravity of the earth.

3. Some people have (travel, traveled) to the moon.

4. Neil Armstrong was (first, the first) man to step on the moon.

5. The moon (shining, shines) beautifully in the night sky.

6. It has (much, many) names such as Luna, Diana, or Artemis.

7. It is also (name, named) by its shape.

Mars is the fourth planet from the Sun in our solar system.

Mars is called "The Red Planet."

This is because the color of its surface is red.

People think that it is a hot planet because of its color.

However, scientists say that Mars is very cold.

Scientists are trying to find out if there are any living things on Mars.

They say Mars has four seasons.

But, the seasons are not the same as those of the earth.

Mars is not so far away from the earth as other planets.

On a clear night, Mars is visible in the sky.

We can see it through a telescope.

---

vocabulary

- planet: 행성
- surface: 표면, 표층(=the face of the earth)
- telescope: 망원경

1. What is Mars known as?

2. Can people live on Mars?

3. What does Mars look like?

1. However, scientists say that Mars is very cold.
   - Nevertheless, scientists say that Mars is very cold.
   - On the contrary, scientists say that Mars is very cold.
   - Despite that, scientists say that Mars is very cold.

2. They say Mars has four seasons.
   - It is said that Mars has four seasons.
   - It is believed that Mars has four seasons.
   - They claim that Mars has four seasons.

3. We can see it through a telescope.
   - We can use a telescope to see it.
   - It can be seen through a telescope.
   - A telescope can be used to see it.

Reorder the following words into correct sentences.

1. This is (of its surface / the color / is red / because).

   _____

2. However, scientist say (that / very / Mars / cold / is).

   _____

3. Scientists are trying to find out (Mars / if / living things / there / any / are / on).

   _____

Choose the correct word or phrase.

1. Mars is (call, called) "The Red Planet."

2. People think it's hot (because, because of) its color.

3. However, scientists (say, saying) that Mars is very cold.

4. They say Mars (have, has) four seasons.

5. But, the seasons are not the same as (that, those) of the earth.

6. Mars is not so (near, far) away from the earth as the other planets.

7. On a clear night, Mars is (visible, invisible) in the sky.

Describe another planet in the solar system.

Jupiter is the fifth planet from the sun in our solar system. It is named after the Roman god Jupiter, also known as Zeus in Greek mythology. Jupiter is made of gas and is the largest planet in our solar system.

To begin, Jupiter is a huge planet. It is one thousandth the mass of the sun, and two and a half times bigger than all the other planets out together. Jupiter has at least 69 moons. The largest of its moons is called Ganamede and is the same size as Mercury.

In addition, Jupiter is called a gas giant. This is because it is made mostly of gas! Jupiter is made of about 90% hydrogen gas and 10% helium gas. You could not stand on Jupiter because there is no ground. Almost the whole planet is just a huge ball of gas.

To summarize, Jupiter is an amazing planet. It is very different from Earth. I would love to become an astronaut and explore Jupiter, but that would be difficult because there is nowhere to stand!

Write a short essay about:

- The solar system

_____

_____

_____

_____

_____

_____

_____

_____

_____

_____

_____

_____

Unit 11

Job

Young learners usually go to school.

They can learn many subjects there.

They also learn how to behave with their teachers and friends.

They learn how to play games.

To learn all these things, they need many teachers.

Teachers know much more about their subjects than students.

Teachers are good at their subjects.

Music teachers are good at singing or playing the piano.

English teachers are good at reading and speaking English.

Math teachers are good with numbers.

Science teachers know a lot about the earth and stars.

Students like their teachers and love to study at school.

Teachers also like their students.

They help their students enjoy going to school.

<u>vocabulary</u>

- behave: 처신하다. 행동하다
- be good at: ~에 능숙하다, ~을 잘한다.

1. What can young students learn at school?

   _____

2. What do your teachers do for you?

   _____

3. What is your English teacher like?

   _____

1. They can learn many subjects there.
   - There, they can learn many subjects.
   - Many subjects can be learned there.
   - There are many subjects they can learn there.

2. Teachers are good at their subjects.
   - Teachers are skilled at their subjects.
   - Teachers are experts at their subjects.
   - Teachers perform in their subjects well.

3. They help their students enjoy going to school.
   - They help their students delight in going to school.
   - They help their students appreciate going to school.
   - They help their students have fun in (going to) school.

Reorder the following words into correct sentences.

1. They learn (games / how / play / to).

   _____

2. Music teachers are (or playing / singing / good at / the piano).

   _____

3. (To / all these / learn / things), they need many teachers.

   _____

Choose the correct word or phrase.

1. Young learners usually (goes, go) to school.

2. They also learn (how to, why to) behave with their teachers and friends.

3. Teachers know (many, much) more about their subjects than students.

4. Teachers are good (for, at) their subjects.

5. English teachers are good at (read, reading) and speaking English.

6. Science teachers know (a lot, a lot of) about the earth and stars.

7. Students like their teachers and love (study, to study) at school.

Many people dream of going to Hollywood.

Most of them want to become famous movie stars.

The life of a movie star is often very exciting.

They meet many interesting people.

They travel to many exciting places and make lots of money.

People think they can enjoy their lives.

However, being a movie star also has a downside.

Movie stars don't have much privacy.

Everything they do is often photographed and talked about by reporters.

Rumors can often make a movie star's life unhappy.

These rumors give them stress and sometimes sadness too.

However, many young people still want to be movie stars.

___

vocabulary

- exciting: 신나는, 흥미진진한(=stimulating)
- rumor: 소문

1. Why do people want to be movie stars?

   _____

2. What do movie stars do?

   _____

3. Why do you think movie stars are not happy?

   _____

1. Most of them want to become famous movie stars.
   - Most of them want to become famous actors or actresses.
   - Most of them want to become well-known movie stars.
   - Most of them want to be renowned celebrities.

2. Movie stars don't have much privacy.
   - Movie stars don't have many secrets.
   - There isn't much privacy in movie stars' lives.
   - Privacy does not really exist in movie stars' lives.

3. However, being a movie star also has a downside.
   - However, being a movie star also has a disadvantage.
   - However, there is also an unpleasant part of being a movie star.
   - However, being a movie has its negative side.

Reorder the following words into correct sentences.

1. Most of them want (to / famous / become / movie / stars).

   _____

2. However, (a movie / being / star / also) has a downside.

   _____

3. (Everything / often / do is / they) photographed and talked about by reporters.

   _____

Choose the correct word or phrase.

1. Many people (dream, dreaming) of going to Hollywood.

2. The life of a movie star is often very (exciting, excited).

3. They meet (much, many) interesting people.

4. People think they can (enjoy, enjoying) their lives a lot.

5. Movie stars don't have (many, much) privacy.

6. Rumors can often (make, made) a movie star's life unhappy.

7. However, many young people still want to (be, are) movie stars.

What is your dream?

My dream is to become a news reporter. I think it is a great job because they can travel the world. Reporters see amazing things and meet interesting people. I will do the following things to get my dream job.

First, I will study national and world news. A reporter must know what is happening in the world. They must have a lot of knowledge about past and current events. I can do this by reading articles in newspapers and online. I can also read books about the past to better understand what is happening now. I should also watch the news broadcast on TV every day.

Second, I should practice my public speaking ability. A reporter must speak confidently and clearly. He must give a lot of details, but also be easy to understand. It takes a lot of practice to be confident speaking in front of people. I will join my school newspaper club and report stories for them to gain experience.

In conclusion, getting your dream job is never easy. We must work hard and be diligent. We must make a plan for the future and do our best to follow it. Being a reporter is my dream and I will make my dream come true!

Write a short essay that answers the question:

- How will you get your dream job?

_____

_____

_____

_____

_____

_____

_____

_____

_____

_____

_____

Unit 12

Sports

Football is a very popular sport all around the world.

Football can be played in two very different ways.

One type of football is called American football.

American football is mostly played in the United States and Canada.

It is a very rough sport involving a lot of physical contact.

The point of the game is to get scores by passing or running with a ball.

The other type of football is also known as soccer.

Soccer is played in almost all countries in the world.

It is less physical than American football.

Each team tries to kick the ball into the other team's net to get scores.

All players must use their feet, head, or chest to play the ball.

Only the goalkeeper is allowed to use their hands, and only within the goal area.

<u>**vocabulary**</u>

- physical contact: 신체접촉
- involve: 수반하다, 포함하다(=imply)

1. What are the two ways to play football?

   _____

2. How does one play American football?

   _____

3. What soccer teams do you know?

   _____

1. Football is a very popular sport all around the world.
   - Football is a beloved sport all around the world.
   - All around the world, football is a very popular sport.
   - Football is played by many people all around the world.

2. It is a very rough sport involving ~~
   - It is a sport that involves force involving ~~
   - It is a sport that requires power involving ~~
   - This sport necessitates strength involving ~~

3. Only the goalkeeper is allowed to use their hands,…
   - Only the goalkeeper is given permission to use their hands,…
   - Only the goalkeeper can use their hands,…
   - Only the goalkeeper is permitted to use their hands,…

Reorder the following words into correct sentences.

1. It is a very rough sport (a lot of / involving / contact / physical).

   _____

2. Soccer is (almost all / played / in / in the world / countries).

   _____

3. The point of the game is (by passing / to get / or running scores / a ball).

   _____

Choose the correct word or phrase.

1. Football is a very popular sport all (around, among) the world.

2. Football can be (play, played) in two very different ways.

3. American football is mostly (play, played) in the United States and Canada.

4. The other type of football is also (know, known) as soccer.

5. It is less physical (to, than) American football.

6. Each team (try, tries) to kick the ball into the other team's net to get scores.

7. One type of football is (calling, called) American football.

The Olympic Games

The Olympic Games are held every four years.

The International Olympic Committee was founded by Pierre de Coubertin in 1894.

The first modern Olympic Games were held in Athens in 1896.

The purpose of Olympics is to maintain peace and unity throughout the whole world with games.

There are two types of Olympic Games: the Winter Olympics and the Summer Olympics, which are held separately.

Athletes from around the world gather for these games.

They compete to see who the best athletes are in the world.

Korea took part in the Olympic Games in 1948 for the first time.

In 1988, the Summer Olympic Games were held in Seoul, Korea.

In 2018, the Winter Olympic Games were held in PyeongChang, Korea.

Korean athletes have won many medals for sports such as taekwondo in summer and short track skating in winter.

---

vocabulary

- hold: 개최하다
- athelete: 운동선수

1. Who founded the IOC?

   _____

2. When did Korea take part in Summer Olympic Games for the first time?

   _____

3. When was the first modern Olympic Games held?

   _____

Substitution Drills

1. The Olympic Games are held every four years.
   - Every four years, the Olympic Games are held.
   - We hold the Olympic Games every four years.
   - Four years pass between each Olympics Games.

2. Athletes from around the world gather for these games.
   - Athletes from countries around the world join these games.
   - These games are joined by international athletes.
   - Athletes across countries participate in these games.

3. Korea took part in the Olympic Games in 1948 for the first time.
   - Korea first took part in the Olympics in 1984.
   - Korea first joined the Olympic Games in 1984.
   - It was in 1984 that Korea first took part in the Olympic Games.

Reorder the following words into correct sentences.

1. The first modern Olympic Games were (in Athens / held / in 1896).

   _____

2. An International Olympic Committee was (Pierre de Coubertin / founded / by / in 1894).

   _____

3. In 1988, the Summer Olympic Games were (Korea / in Seoul / held).

   _____

Sentence Check

Choose the correct word or phrase.

1. The Olympic games are (hold, held) every four years.

2. There are two (type, types) of Olympic Games.

3. Athletes (from, for) around the world gather for these games.

4. They compete to (see, seeing) who the best athletes are in the world.

5. Korea first (take, took) part in the Olympic Games in 1948.

6. In 2018, the Winter Olympic Games (was, were) held in PyeongChang, Korea.

7. Korean athletes have (win, won) many medals for sports.

What are sports?

Sports are enjoyed by people of all ages all over the world. Many of us like to watch sports on TV or go to a live game. We cheer for our favorite team and celebrate when they win. Sports improve our lives in a lot of ways.

For starters, sports can be a great hobby. We can play sports with our friends. We can watch our favorite sports after school or on the weekend. Fans collect sports cards and team uniforms to show their team spirit. We can talk about our favorite players and teams with our friends.

Next, sports can give us national pride. There are many international sporting events like the FIFA World Cup or the Olympic Games. In Korea, thousands of people gather to watch these games together and show support for their country. When Korea does well, it makes everyone very happy and proud!

In conclusion, sports can be a big part of our everyday lives. We can have a lot of fun and also it brings people closer together. I think we should all realize how important sports are.

Go, team, go!

Write a short essay that answers the question.

- How do sports improve our lives?

_____

_____

_____

_____

_____

_____

_____

_____

_____

_____

_____

_____

_____

Unit 13

Capital Cities

Lesson 1 Seoul

Seoul is the capital of South Korea.

It is one of the largest cities in the world.

Seoul has about 10 million people.

It is home to about 20% of the Korean population.

Seoul has a lot of historical buildings, including several palaces.

It has many tall buildings and big companies.

The city lies on the banks of the Han River.

It divides the city into two parts – Gangnam and Gangbuk.

Traffic jams are a big problem in Seoul.

Air pollution is another big problem.

Car companies are trying to produce small sized cars.

Some car companies are developing electric cars to reduce air pollution.

They want to reduce or even to stop air pollution and save the world.

vocabulary

- capital: 수도
- million: 백만
- pollution: 오염

1. What is the population of Seoul?

_____

2. What are the some of the big problem in Seoul?

_____

3. Why do car companies try to produce electric cars?

_____

1. Seoul is the capital of South Korea.
   - The capital of South Korea is Seoul.
   - The city of Seoul is a metropolis in South Korea.
   - The economic center of South Korea is in Seoul.

2. Seoul has about 10 million people.
   - Seoul has approximately 10 million people.
   - Seoul has close to 10 million people.
   - There are about 10 million people in Seoul.

3. The city lies on the banks of the Han River.
   - The city sits on the banks of the Han River.
   - The city surrounds the Han River
   - The city surrounds the Han River.
   - The city is located alongside the Han River.

Reorder the following words into correct sentences.

1. It is (the largest / cities / one of / in the world).

   _____

2. It is (of the Korean / home to / population / about 20%).

   _____

3. Traffic jams are (in / a big / Seoul / problem).

   _____

Choose the correct word or phrase.

1. Seoul is the capital (from, of) Korea.

2. Seoul has (about, for) 10 million people.

3. The city lies (at, on) the banks of the Han River.

4. It divides the city (from, into) two parts – Gangnam and Gangbuk.

5. Car companies are trying (producing, to produce) small sized cars.

6. Some car companies are (develop, developing) electric cars to reduce air pollution.

7. They want to stop air pollution and (saving, save) the world.

Washington, D.C. is the capital of the United States of America.

However, it is not the largest city in the USA.

The city has the national government, which includes the White House.

The president of the United States lives in this house.

New York City was the capital city of America before the 1800s.

However, New York City was too big and too far north.

George Washington, the first president of the USA, suggested moving the capital city to another place.

They set up government buildings there.

They named the city Washington, D.C.

Washington, D.C. was named after George Washington.

He was also a general in the American Army.

This city now has around 681,000 people.

---

vocabulary

- White House: 백악관
- include: 포함하다

1. Which was the first capital city of America?

   _____

2. Why was the city named Washington, D.C.?

   _____

3. What do you think D.C. stands for?

   _____

1. The president of the United States lives in this house.
   - This house is where the the president of the United States lives.
   - The president of the United States resides in this house.
   - This is the home of the US president.

2. They set up government buildings there.
   - They built government buildings there.
   - They established government buildings there.
   - Government buildings were set up there.

3. They named the city Washington, D.C.
   - They called the city Washington, D.C.
   - They christened the city Washington, D.C.
   - The city was named Washington, D.C.

Reorder the following words into correct sentences.

1. The president of the United States (this / lives / house / in).

   _____

2. They set (government / up / there / buildings).

   _____

3. The city has the national government, (the White House / includes / which).

   _____

Sentence Check

Choose the correct word or phrase.

1. However, it is not the largest city (in, about) the USA.

2. New York City (is, was) the original capital city of America before the 1800s.

3. George Washington suggested (move, moving) the capital city to another place.

4. They (were named, named) the city Washington, D.C.

5. Washington, D.C. was named (in, after) George Washington.

6. He (were, was) also a general in the American Army.

7. This city now (have, has) around 681,000 people.

What is Canada's capital city?

Many people know Canada as a large country with beautiful nature. They know about ice hockey and maple syrup. They know that Vancouver and Toronto are big and exciting cities. However, a lot of people don't know that the capital city of Canada is Ottawa.

To begin, Ottawa is in a great location. It is in the province of Ontario next to the Ottawa River. The river connects to the five great lakes of Canada, which are the biggest lakes in the world. The Hudson Bay and Niagara Falls are also nearby. It is a short drive to great cities such as Toronto and Montreal. Also, it is quite close to the American border, so it is easy to visit the United States.

Additionally, Ottawa is a center for Canadian culture. The national parliament buildings are located on Parliament Hill in downtown Ottawa. This is the center of the Canadian government. Also, there are many museums and art galleries. The city is very multi-cultural and many people speak both official languages of Canada, which are English and French.

In conclusion, not only is Ottawa the capital city of Canada, it is a great city. It is located in the central area near many attractions and the perfect place to learn about Canadian culture. I am sure that it is one of the best places to visit and live in Canada.

Write a short essay about the following:

- Tell me about another capital city.

_____

_____

_____

_____

_____

_____

_____

_____

_____

_____

_____

_____

_____

Unit 14

Public Announcements

Ladies and gentlemen!

This is your captain, Daniel Park, speaking.

Welcome to Flight AC 064, leaving Incheon Airport and arriving in Vancouver, Canada.

Our flight will be about 11 hours.

We will be flying at 34,000 feet.

We ask that you do the following for your safety and comfort during the flight.

Please keep your seatbelt fastened until the captain has turned off the signs.

And, keep your carry-on items in the overhead bins.

Please turn off your portable electronic devices.

Smoking will not be allowed in the aircraft.

Thank you for choosing our airline and have a good flight.

<u>**vocabulary**</u>

- seatbelt: 안전벨트
- cabin: (항공기의) 선실, 보관하는 곳

1. Where will the flight leave for?

   _____

2. When can the passengers unbuckle their seatbelt?

   _____

3. List some instructions given by the captain.

   _____

Substitution Drills

1. Welcome to Flight AC 064, leaving Incheon Airport...
   - Welcome to Flight AC 064, departing from Incheon Airport...
   - Welcome to Flight AC 064, taking off from Incheon Airport...
   - Welcome to Flight AC 064, flying from Incheon Airport...

2. ...arriving in Vancouver, Canada.
   - ...landing in Vancouver, Canada.
   - ...going to Vancouver, Canada.
   - ...deplaning in Vancouver, Canada.

3. Smoking will not be allowed in the aircraft.
   - Smoking will be prohibited in the aircraft.
   - It is not allowed to smoke in the aircraft.
   - No one is permitted to smoke in the aircraft.

Reorder the following words into correct sentences.

1. Please turn off (your / off / electronic / devices / portable).

    _____

2. Thank you for (our airline / choosing / a good flight / and have)

    _____

3. (Flight / Welcome to / AC 064,) leaving Incheon airport and arriving in Vancouver).

    _____

Choose the correct word or phrase.

1. Our flight will (being, be) about 11 hours.

2. We ask that you do the following (in, for) your safety and comfort during the flight.

3. Please keep your seatbelt (fasten, fastened) until the captain has turned off the signs.

4. And keep your carry-on items (out of, in) the overhead bins.

5. Please turn (at, off) your portable electronic devices.

6. Smoking will not be allowed (on, in) the aircraft.

7. We will be flying (for, at) 34,000 feet.

This is the weekend weather forecast for Seoul from July 28th to 29th.

Get ready for increasingly high temperatures as the summer heat will not stop.

Saturday will have a mid-day high of 32 degrees Celsius and a low of 21 degrees Celsius at night.

The skies will be clear and the sun will be shining brightly.

Make sure to put on some sun block if you're going outside.

Sunday will be more of the same, with a high of 31 and a low of 20.

It will be humid all weekend, so look forward to some sweat.

It is not advisable to play sports.

But, doing the laundry and hanging it out to dry will be a good idea.

The best option for this weekend, however, might be to stay home and keep the air conditioning on high!

---

vocabulary

- temperature: 온도
- advisable: 권할만한, 바람직한

1. How will the weather be on Saturday?

   _____

2. What should you do before going out at day time?

   _____

3. What is the best option for this weekend?

   _____

1. Get ready for increasingly high temperatures…
   - Get ready for progressively high temperatures…
   - Get ready for highr temperatures…
   - Get ready for more and more high temperatures…

2. The skies will be clear…
   - There will be clear skies…
   - Clear skies will be expected…
   - There will be no clouds in the skies…

3. It is not advisable at all to play some sports.
   - It is not a good idea to play some sports.
   - It is best not to play sports.
   - Playing sports is not a smart idea.

Reorder the following words into correct sentences.

1. Sunday will (be / the same / more / of).

   _____

2. The skies will be clear and (will be / brightly / the sun / shining).

   _____

3. Make sure to (put on / sun block / if / some) you're going outside.

   _____

Choose the correct word or phrase.

1. This is the weekend weather forecast (by, for) Seoul from July 28th to 29th.

2. Get ready (in, for) increasingly high temperatures as the summer heat will not stop.

3. Saturday will (has, have) a mid-day high of 32 degrees Celsius.

4. The skies will (is, be) clear and the sun will be shining brightly.

5. Make sure to (put, puts) on some sun block if you're going outside.

6. It will (is, be) humid all weekend so look forward to some sweat.

7. The best option for this weekend might be (to stay, stay) home.

Class Rules

Hello my fellow students! I am your class mate, Kim Sae-ra. I hope you are having a good day and studying English very hard. Now, I will tell you about our English classroom rules.

First, we must only speak English in the classroom. Our teacher is from Australia, so we must always try to speak English with her. It is difficult to find a chance to speak English in Korea, so take this opportunity and do your best.

Second, we must never use our cell phone in class. Many of our friends send us text messages and mobile games are very fun, but we cannot be distracted during class. We must focus and always pay attention to the teacher.

In closing, I want to say thank you for listening to my announcement. Please try to follow these rules and study hard. Our teacher is very smart and kind. If we study hard and follow the rules, we can learn many things!

Write a short essay about:

- An announcement of your English classroom rules

_____

_____

_____

_____

_____

_____

_____

_____

_____

_____

_____

_____

_____

_____

_____

_____

_____

_____

_____

_____

_____

Teacher's Comment